# WALKS AROUND KESWICK

## 10 WALKS UNDER 6 MILES

C000008535

DALESMAN

**Dalesman Publishing Company Ltd**
Stable Courtyard, Broughton Hall,
Skipton, North Yorkshire BD23 3AE


**First Edition 1997**
**Reprinted 2000**

A British Library Cataloguing in Publication record
is available for this book


**ISBN 1 85568 119 6**

Printed by Amadeus Press, Cleckheaton, West Yorkshire

# Contents

# Introduction

Keswick, the capital of the Northern Lake District, has everything for everyone. Gentle strolls, full day mountain expeditions and hundreds of rock climbs. There's an abundance of outdoor shops and gift shops, a variety of splendid tearooms and friendly hostelries that don't mind muddy boots and wellies. Many visitors enjoy exploring the fells and valleys around Keswick. However, the weather can change from blue, sunny skies to black rainclouds within a very short time, so make sure you've got some warm, waterproof clothing with you, even in the valleys.

The town was granted its market charter in the 13th century. By the middle of the 16th century wool was no longer the main industry. Mining had hit the area and the huge Goldscope Mine in the Newlands Valley was the first to be opened by Queen Elizabeth I's newly formed Company of the Mines Royal. A century later graphite was mined on a large scale. This was used to make cannon balls among other things. The interest in graphite continues today in the form of Keswick's ever-popular Cumberland Pencil Museum.

In the late 18th century the Victorians brought tourism to Keswick. This is still the most important income to the town today and any visitor can understand why. Nestled between Lakeland's fourth highest mountain, Skiddaw, and the vast blue expanse of Derwent Water, Keswick's natural splendour and space is admired by all.

The wettest place in England is just down the valley, a hamlet called Seathwaite, so Keswick is prepared. The Tourist Information Centre in the central building of the historical Moot Hall is teeming with tips and ideas. Also, make use of the excellent National Park Information Centre located on the lake road. Local knowledge abounds at both centres.

# Langstrath Valley

**This classic valley walk combines the peace of the hills with the excitement of rocky streams and waterfalls. Wellies are recommended for any watery explorations. Level paths on stones or grass; possibility of boggy sections on second half of walk.**
**Length of walk: 4 miles.**
**Start/finish: Car park at Rosthwaite in Borrowdale.**

Follow the lane right from the car park. It bends sharply left, right and left again. Walk past two or three cottages and take a small, walled lane on the right after Clare's Cottage and an adjacent garage. A few yards on the left, a sign-post leads you through a gate towards Longthwaite Youth Hostel.

Walk across the field and over a stile at the end. Follow the path diagonally right and through a gate. A yellow arrow on the gate sends you left to another gate by some white cottages. Follow the narrow footpath between the buildings and through a gate to a metalled lane. Turn left and follow the lane for a few hundred yards to the main B5289 road. Cross this road carefully and continue ahead on another lane. This meanders past a small row of white cottages and Borrowdale School on the right and soon enters the tiny village of Stonethwaite. Continue along the lane through the village.

A few yards beyond Langstrath Country Hotel, towards the end of the village, go through a large gate on the left which has a sign saying No Vehicles next to a Public Footpath finger-post. The stony track crosses two small fields and a larger, more open one. Go over the ladder stile at the end of the larger field to walk through a sparse wood with Stonethwaite Beck flowing about 50 yards to your left.

A small, fenced-in wood soon appears on your right. This houses the toilet block for Stonethwaite campsite ahead. Follow the track beside it and, where the wire fence corners and turns right, around the wood, take a faint path ahead for about 100 yards. You will then hit the main stony track again.

As you pass a larger enclosed wood on the right, the path becomes rockier and climbs up to a ladder stile in the stone wall ahead. Beyond this stile the short, rocky descent crosses a small beck and continues ahead with a wire fence and

Stonethwaite Beck on your left. The magnificent steep, curving ridge to your left leads over Coldbarrow Fell and onto the 2370ft summit of Ullscarf.

The path goes over another stile. To the left are rocky pools and waterfalls waiting to be explored. However, take care, especially after heavy rain, as the water races along at an amazing speed. After your exploration, head back to the stile and take the path that leads from it to a stone wall on the right, away from the waterfalls. It soon passes around the end of the wall and through a few scattered trees. The path swings right at a wire fence and becomes wide and stony with a different beck, Langstrath, now to your left.

Pass through a gate and continue along the Langstrath valley for a few hundred yards until you see a footbridge spanning the water. Walk across this and turn left on the opposite bank of the beck. Above, Eagle Crag rises from the fellside. You may see a few climbers on it. This leads up and back to the 2,500ft High Raise, Lakeland's central fell.

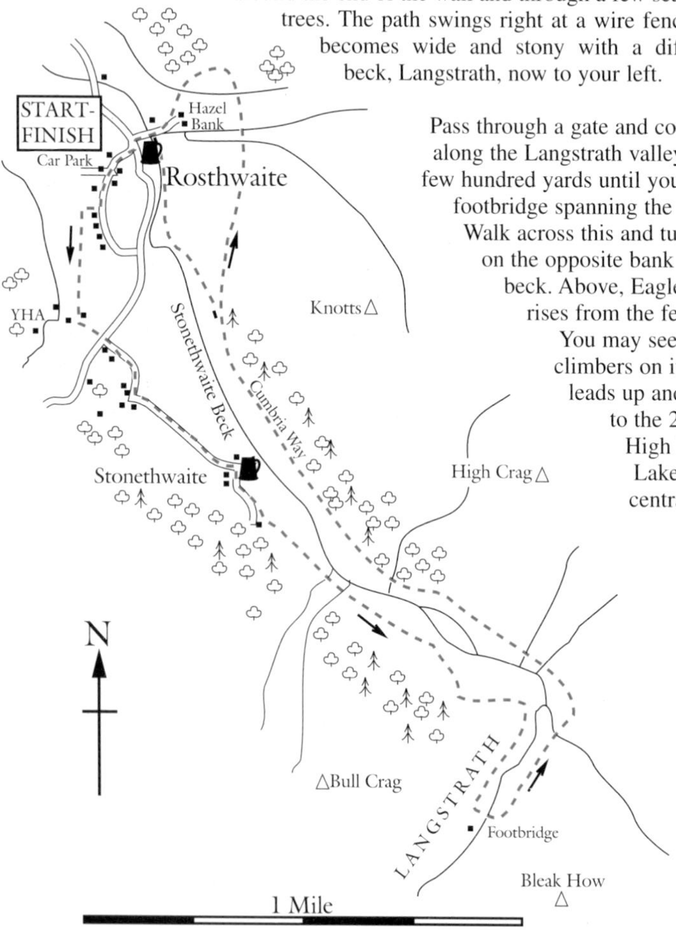

START-FINISH

Car Park

Hazel Bank

Rosthwaite

YHA

Stonethwaite Beck

Cumbria Way

Knotts △

High Crag △

Stonethwaite

N

△ Bull Crag

LANGSTRATH

Footbridge

Bleak How △

1 Mile

Our path follows a stone wall to the left with the beck beyond and you soon go through a gate. As you walk near the water's edge, there are more rocks and waterfalls to explore. The path alternates between grass, stones and bogs as it follows Langstrath Beck. The beck soon loses itself to Stonethwaite Beck near where you cross another footbridge. The water below the bridge is Greenup Gill and it, too, is soon swallowed up by Stonethwaite Beck a little further downstream.

Go through a gate ahead and turn left on a well defined stony footpath. After a few hundred yards you pass some large black gates on the left with Galleny Force on the right. Cross this waterfall over the path and go through a gate. A stone wall now lies on your left with a tumbledown stone wall on your right. The path soon leads through another gate, becoming grassy underfoot, then you walk over a small footbridge. Keep to the left path that continues to hug the wall. The fellside to the right is covered with woodland.

Follow the path through another gate by an old, rusty sign-post. The path zig-zags through another gate. Ignore the track to Stonethwaite on the left. Continue ahead on a public bridleway sign-posted Watendlath via Rosthwaite. Go through another gate and soon pass a slate sign on the left wall confirming that you are still on the path to Rosthwaite.

After the path swings right and then twice left you come to a gate. The path through this gate follows a riverbank, eventually turning left over a bridge. You can then cross the main road back to the carpark. If you're well shod and are in the mood for a last little adventure with amazing views, don't pass through the gate. Instead, take the faint green path to the right approximately 50 yards before this, by a large tree on the last bend. This quickly leads to a gate in a stonewall ahead and the path becomes more obvious as you go through the gate and continue ahead. A stonewall is on your left.

You soon pass over two water channels in the fellside. The path gently undulates before climbing to cross a beck by a large holly tree and then leads through a gate. It becomes steeper and passes a slate sign directing you upwards and onwards towards Watendlath and Rosthwaite. Across a small beck you soon descend through a gate in the wall ahead. After the next beck the path sweeps gently ahead. About 10 yards after another beck, go through a gate on the left. A sign-post confirms that you've just come from the direction of Stonethwaite.

The wide, stony track zig-zags downhill fairly steeply so take care. Near the bottom go through a gate and over the two water channels that you saw higher on the fellside. This track becomes a narrow path and leads to a metalled lane. Turn right on this and go over the bridge to the main B5289 road. Cross this carefully and walk left for a few yards before turning right down the lane back to the car park.

# Cat Bells and Derwent Water

**This walk is generally regarded as a classic of Keswick. You may choose to start the outing from across the lake at Keswick by catching a ferry over to Hawes End. Remember to check return times. Mostly wide easy tracks across fell and woodland. Length of walk: 4½ miles. Start/finish: Hawes End car park on road from Portinscale to Grange.**

If you're not including a ferry ride in you itinerary, walk over the cattlegrid up the lane from the parking area and turn directly left on an obvious footpath uphill. This brings you to a lane. Walk left along this for a few yards before turning right on a wide public bridleway that heads diagonally left up the fellside of Cat Bells. There is a National Trust sign here that re-routes walkers doing the Cat Bells ridge. You are walking along Cat Bells' lower terrace path so this doesn't refer to you.

You soon have splendid views over Keswick and Derwent Water. Directly across the lake, over a mile away, lie Castlerigg Fell and Bleaberry Fell. Ahead is the popular walking and climbing valley of Borrowdale. The humps of Cat Bells soon appear above you on the right. The broad path narrows as you walk close to gorse bushes then soon widens again. There is a bench just past this and then the path starts to descend gradually. At the road walk across a small parking lay-by. The path then continues ahead up the fellside on a wide, gravelled track. Follow the path on an easy gradient as you pass above two obvious bays in the lake, Brandelhow and Abbot's Bays. A little further on, past some National Trust fencing, you pass above a large house named Brackenburn.

A stone bench lies ahead near a slate plaque in the rock. This is in memory of Sir Hugh Walpole of Brackenburn, author of, among other things, four famous novels that formed the Herries Chronicles between 1930 and 1933. These told of the changes and fortunes of a Cumberland family spanning 200 years. His visitors included several well known writers such as J. B. Priestley, W. H. Auden and Arthur Ransome. You soon pass some more buildings on the left and then a stone wall runs alongside the path with a deciduous wood beyond it. Stay on this path, ignoring another one that forks diagonally up the fellside.

The wall soon leaves the path as you continue downhill. The path widens and passes a stony track on the right next to a National Trust sign for Cat Bells. Go through the gate at the bottom and turn right on the permitted footpath to Hollows Farm and Seatoller. This drops down to the road where you turn right again.

Continue past Manesty Holiday Cottages and Youdale Knott on the right. Just before a house on the left there is a large gate on the left. An old, rusty finger-post points across the field to Lodore. Although Lodore isn't our destination, go through the gate and onto the farm track with Eller's Beck on your right. Cat Bells is now ahead and to the left with the craggy facade of Maiden Moor looming closer on your left. After about 150 yards the beck veers off to the right. Stay on the wide track, go over a footbridge and soon through a kissing gate. There is a wood on the left as the track leads through another kissing gate.

Follow the obvious green path diagonally left. After about 100 yards Derwent Water comes into view again and there is a small crossroads. Take the narrow path to the right heading directly for the lake through grass and bracken. The path comes to a T-junction near the water's edge. Turn left along a grassy path that soon passes over boardwalks before continuing ahead on a stony path. The harsh sound of your feet on the boardwalks cuts through the quietness of your surroundings.

The lake disappears from view. At a fork go either way as both paths soon meet up again. Walk across another boardwalk to a gate in a stonewall. Through this gate follow the obvious track through Manesty Wood with the lake close on your right again. There are a few footbridges ahead to keep your feet dry and then the path traverses left away from the shore. You soon rejoin the lakeside over another footbridge. To your right lies Abbot's Bay which you could see from Cat Bells' terrace path. The views across the lake to Blencathra in the far distance are superb from here. The path comes to a slate bungalow called The Warren where you turn right on a small lane. Ahead you can see a wooden bench overlooking the lake.

Turn left at the bench on to another lane. This leads through a gate. A footpath veers right past a house called Brandelhow. The bay of the same name lies to your right as you walk over a footbridge towards a fenced-in wood. Climb up the bank ahead with the fence on your right and go through a small gate and into the wood. Walk along the wide track ahead and continue following the lakeside path as it passes a ferry landing stage.

The path is easy to follow and you have the lake close to your right all the way through the woods. Walk past Withesike Bay and then, at Victoria Bay, the path by-passes a promontory. There is another landing stage just beyond this bay where the woods end. Go through the gate in the wall next to it and turn left on a wide path. The lake is now behind you. This path continues ahead through pasture land. It soon passes through an iron gate with a building on the left. The lake returns on your right. This is Otterbield Bay, "the sheltering place of the otter".

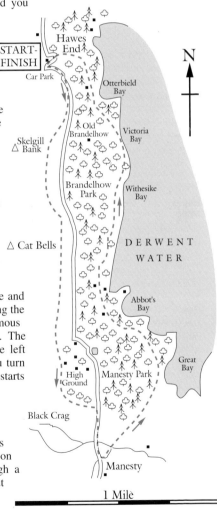

The path continues up to a gate and onto a lane. Turn right, following the sign for Lingholm (which is famous for its gardens) and Keswick. The lane passes Hawes End on the left and, just past the building, you turn right. The lane sweeps left then starts to swing right with Derwent Bay Woodcrafts on the right. Opposite this is a finger-post sign. Turn left here on the public footpath towards Cat Bells with a stone wall on your right. This passes through a small wood and brings you out at the parking area near the cattlegrid.

Walk 3

# Cat Bells and Newlands

**For relatively little effort, this walk offers incredible views over the
Newlands Valley and its much-traversed mountains.
Mostly level footpaths, tracks and lanes.
Length of walk: 4½ miles.
Start/finish: Hawes End car park on the Portinscale to Grange road.**

You should be able to park at the main parking area under the trees at a wide zig-zag just beyond Hawes End. There is additional parking further on, 150 yards past a cattlegrid, but this is a smaller area and usually full. From the main parking area follow the lane up and over the cattlegrid. At a sharp left bend fork off to the right and continue following this lane for about a third of a mile. The lane leads to the ancient sheep farm at Skelgill. The return journey will bring you through the farm buildings and the gate on the right but for now go through the large gate to the left onto a wide, rough track by a footpath sign. This track climbs diagonally left away from the farm.

There are soon magnificent views to the right. Straight across the valley the easily identified knobbly summit of Causey Pike lies to the left of the rolling highland ridge that leads up to Grisedale Pike. As you continue along the track you will see the square bulk of Robinson ahead to the right a little. Above your head, to the left, loom the obvious humps of Cat Bells. The name may be a corruption of Cat Bields, "the shelter of the wildcat." You may see the odd farm cat today, but nothing more wild, only the silhouettes of rambling groups as they trudge up the ridge.

Ignore any tempting green paths to the left which head up to the summit of Cat Bells. Continue following the track as its steepness soon gives way to a very gradual incline with a stone wall on your right. After walking along this track for about half a mile you come to some now abandoned mining levels. From the 13th century the area around Newlands was mined for gold, silver, copper and lead and there is plenty of evidence of this bygone age in the disused mines scattered about the valley.

Follow the same track through the levels. It soon veers off left to follow the steep bank of Yewthwaite Gill for a few yards, past a National Trust sign warning of mining subsidence. You then ford the gill at a wide, shallow

11

crossing and continue on the obvious path ahead to a stone wall on your right. The path widens as it hugs the wall.

Below, the tiny village of Little Town soon comes into view. At a right hairpin bend by a small clump of tall trees near the village road, take the faint green path off the bend to your left. This drops down to a wide, stony track and you can now see and hear Newlands Beck to the right. You now have ample opportunities to soak up the wonderful views around you as the next mile or so is easy as you follow the track with a stone wall on your right.

The wall then turns sharp right and the valley bottom is a few yards away on the right. Here, turn right with the wall and walk across a footbridge over Newlands Beck and through a small gate ahead. The path hugs the wall for about 100 yards before fording a small beck and heading up a short steeper section to a gravel track. Turn right on the track. Above and to the left is Scope End with the ruins of Goldscope Mine on its flank. This is one of the oldest and richest mines in the valley, first mined in the middle of the 16th century by German miners who settled here.

Follow the track to Low Snab Farm on your right. Go through the large gate, along the permissive footpath through the farmyard and out onto the driveway. Through the next gate the lane leads over Scope Beck and swings to the right to end in front of the tiny whitewashed Newlands Church. Turn right at the church on a metalled lane and then right again at a T-junction. You pass back over Newlands Beck before climbing up the lane and into the village of Little Town. This is where Beatrix Potter set one of her many classic children's stories, The Tale of Mrs. Tiggy-Winkle.

Opposite Little Town Farm on the left at the end of the village, a finger-post sends you ahead 50 yards to turn right down a walled lane. Pass through a gate at the end and continue along the lane and over a small footbridge as the track bears left. It meanders between hedges, fences and walls. After passing through a gate the track leads to a second gate by a small cottage. Go through this and follow the obvious path diagonally right behind the building. You're soon walking on a grassy path through a field. Skiddaw looms ahead on the skyline with the bald-headed Swinside in front.

At the far end of the field go through a kissing gate and continue ahead with bushy trees on your left and open fellside to your right, to a ladder stile. Go over this and follow the path ahead over three more stiles. Almost directly beyond the third one the path leads between farm buildings and through a large gate to a metalled lane. Turn right here, passing in front of Skelgill Farm, and up to another gate. Here you will have a little deja-vu. All that remains is for you to follow the lane back to the car.

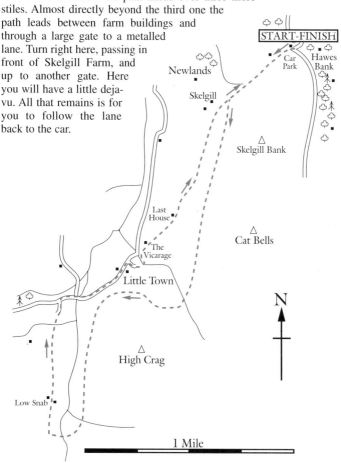

# Castle Head and Great Wood

**This walk combines peaceful woodland with the refreshing, open
shores of Derwent Water and takes in an impressive viewpoint.
Mostly level but with a few short, steeper sections; well-maintained
grassy and rocky paths.
Length of walk: 4 miles.
Start/finish: Keswick Lakeside car park.**

Leave the Keswick Lakeside car park by the entrance near the public
telephone. Just past the Keswick Mountain Rescue base turn right and walk
along a path between two hedges. Go across the road and onto a metalled
path before crossing another road to a pavement. Turn right along the
pavement, past about four large driveways and two seats set into the stone
wall. After about 200 yards, go through a gap in the wall on the left signposted public footpath and National Trust Castle Head.

Follow the path up through the woods. Just as the path starts to descend
there is another path to the right with an old, wide tree trunk guarding its
entrance under overhanging branches. Follow this right-hand path to the top
of Castle Head, taking care on the rocks as they can be slippery when wet.
Superb views greet you, encompassing all that the Lake District has to offer.
Pastures, wooded slopes, shimmering water, craggy outcrops of rock and
stark, barren mountainsides are all on show here. There is a marker
identifying the points on the horizon.

For many people Cat Bells dominates the landscape from this viewpoint. Its
deceptively sharp-looking humps seem to rise sheer from the water's edge.
In reality it offers a pleasant afternoon stroll and is the perfect introduction
to higher fell walking. Back-track to the tree stump and turn right on the
main path to descend out of the woods through a kissing-gate. The path then
leads to a quiet, residential road where you turn right. Follow this until you
come to Springs Farm on the right by a bridge. The road becomes a track as
you walk through the farmyard and outbuildings to a gate.

Continue through the gate and up through woodland with a stream on your
left. At a junction, just before a footbridge, turn right following a sign
towards Rakefoot Farm, Walla Crag and Castlerigg Stone Circle. There are

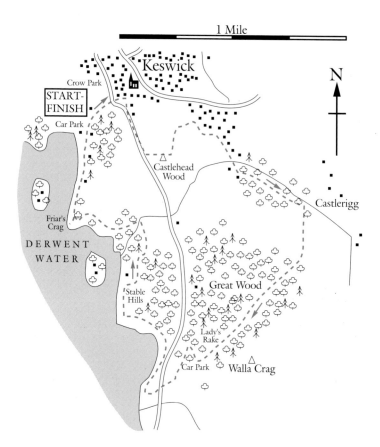

magnificent views over Derwent Water as you wend your way up by the side of a wood and past a large aerial.

Turn right in front of a stile and gate and follow the narrow path that leads over a stile and into Great Wood. The wooden block to the left of the stile lifts to allow dogs in. Take a few minutes to look back over Keswick and its beautiful setting. Once inside the wood, follow the path straight ahead and just keep going. If you're very quiet and just a little lucky, you may see deer grazing. Just over halfway through Great Wood the trees open up on the left giving stunning views up to Walla Crag. Soon afterwards you can see Derwent Water through the trees ahead.

The path descends more steeply to a T-junction where you turn right, following the path as it veers left and enters the National Trust's Great Wood car park. Beyond the gate walk diagonally left to the car park exit and follow this lane to the main road. This is another good vantage point for fresh views of Walla Crag. Take care as you cross the road to another footpath through a wall. It's sign-posted National Trust Calf Close Bay and you can clearly see the water ahead as you walk down the path through the trees. At the shore turn right on the footpath. The path doesn't stray very far from the shoreline and you soon come to a short, steep section that climbs over tree roots. Above this, a bench offers a welcome rest. Continue on this path to a large stone pillar which is a collection box for National Trust donations. There's a fork in the path here so make sure you stay on the left path as you pass the pillar. The bay gives brilliant views across to the fells.

Follow the path across a small footbridge and around the bay. Just past another well-placed bench, you walk through a small wood and then a gate. Follow the clear footpath with open pasture to the right and the shore on your left. The path becomes a gravel drive as you pass the buildings on the left called Stable Hills. At a cattle grid continue ahead on what is now a metalled lane. The lane soon curves to the right. At this bend you will see a short gravel track that leads down to a gate in the wall on the left. Walk through the gate and follow the path through woodland. You will soon see Derwentwater ahead before emerging at a gate. Go through this gate and continue on the path to the lakeside.

From the shore pass through a gate into a small wood. Turn left up rock steps and spend some time exploring Friar's Crag. In the 7th Century, friars gathered here to be blessed by St Herbert who lived on nearby St Herbert's Island. There is also a memorial to John Ruskin, Victorian artist, writer and active campaigner of social causes. His final home, Brantwood at Coniston, attracts many visitors. Exploration complete, continue on the main path, past a memorial to Canon Rawnsley, co-founder of the Lake District's largest land owner, the National Trust. The path soon becomes a metalled road leading back to the car park past the landing stages and a well-positioned tea room.

# Whinlatter Forest Park

**This is an exploration of England's only mountain forest and one of the Forestry Commission's oldest forests.**
**Mostly clear forest tracks; some smaller, easy to follow footpaths.**
**Length of walk: 4½ miles.**
**Start/finish: Whinlatter Forest Park Visitor Centre car park on the B5292 from Braithwaite.**

From the main car park walk up to the visitor centre. The shop and tearoom will still be there after your walk so save them for later. There is another path here that leads left, away from the centre. Walk along this, popping into the huge badger sett on the right to reappear a few yards further down. Next to the exit hole there is a finger-post pointing right to the trail so take this gravel path. Follow it upwards, past the children's play area on your left and continue following the red, blue and green waymarkers. You soon cross a footbridge over a beck. A selection of wire fences lie just beyond this and a sign on the right explains about Tree Munchers and the fences.

Continue climbing through the wood to a superb viewpoint with illustrated information boards about the views. Follow the green waymarked path ahead and climb quite steeply through the evergreen woods. At a wide forest track turn left. Ahead is another splendid viewpoint complete with bench and information board. This looks out to Grisedale Pike which, at 2,593ft high, is conspicuous from many points around the area. Take the wide gravelled path directly to the right of the sign and descend gradually. Grisedale Pike soon disappears behind the trees. The path leads to the main B5292 road which you cross carefully. Follow the footpath opposite through some trees with a stone wall soon appearing on your left. Walk across a small footbridge and continue on the path as it passes behind the wall so that the wall is now on your right.

You soon climb some steps to a forest road. Turn left here and continue to another forest road. Turn left again. This drops down gradually before passing over Grisedale Beck and then climbs up to a large forest gate. Beyond this turn right following the lane as it then sweeps left with a car park and wooden building on the right. Go through another gate and up the forest road. At the next T-junction, turn left. Grisedale Pike comes back into view behind you.

You soon pass a broad grassy track on the left with good views of Skiddaw beyond it. Continue ahead on the main track until, after about 200 yards, this track forks. A post here tells you that this is junction number 45. Take the right track and climb steadily up. At a right hand bend, take a grassy, gravelled track that leads down to the left over Hospital Plantation which you viewed near the start of the walk.

After about a quarter of a mile you will see a three-foot-high, square post on the left. Turn left here onto a more overgrown track with overhanging trees. Descend to an open stretch of land with wonderful views. Causey Pike is directly ahead with its pink scree run down the middle. Left of this and in front of it lies Stile End with Barrow a little further left. You walk between these two hills on the Coledale and Barrow Door walk later in this book.

You soon reach a wide forest track where you turn left through the pine forest again. Continue descending gradually, ignoring a right turn at junction 48. You are now walking in a deciduous wood. The track then comes to a wider forest road with a large hairpin bend in it. Take the right hand option which continues almost straight ahead. Descend along this gradually, ignoring another forest track that soon appears on your right. Skiddaw looms ahead and to the right.

Continue on the track for about a third of a mile, until it climbs up and swings left on a wide, sweeping bend. You will see the B5292 below to your right beyond the trees. As you come out of this bend, where the track becomes straight again, there is a faint path that leads off to the right and zig-zags down for about 30 yards to the road. Cross the road and go through the large gate directly ahead to walk along another forest road. This soon bends left and there are good views over to Skiddaw and the end of Bassenthwaite Lake to your right, with Thornthwaite Forest ahead.

Ignore a forest track to the right. The road soon turns left by a telegraph pole.

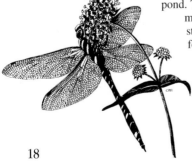

Take the small path to the right, by the pole, and enjoy a peaceful rest by a small tarn, or pond. This area is Comb Beck and is home to many forest animals including heron, stoat and newt. The path continues ahead for a few yards with the tarn on your left. You then have a choice. Either cross an outlet of the tarn and then head directly down to the right on a small path to cross Comb Beck stream a few yards further on. Or,

18

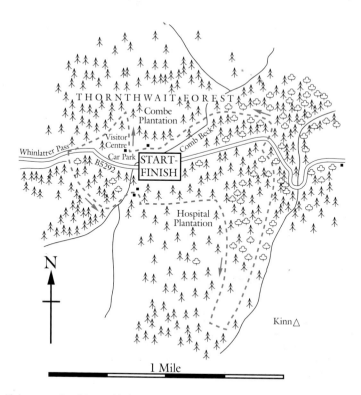

N

1 Mile

if the water level is too high to cross, retrace your steps past the bench back to the track and turn right. If you take the second option, turn left at the next junction and follow that track for about half a mile back to the visitor centre.

However, if the water level is acceptable and you have crossed both streams, continue up the opposite bank and follow a blue waymarker ahead. This path climbs up to a colourful information board about Comb Beck and its inhabitants. From here, the path continues through the woods for a few hundred yards following the blue markers until you drop down left to a forest road. Cross this diagonally right and take the small path ahead, still following the blue markers. Continue up through a wood which can be muddy underfoot. Towards the end of this wood the path runs close to a stone wall on the left. As you come out onto a broad forest road turn left, still following the blue markers. This road soon returns you to the visitor centre where the shop, tearoom and play area await.

# Castlerigg and Naddle Valley

**Imaginations can run wild on this interesting walk steeped in history.
Good paths and lanes; gently undulating with a few short, steep sections
Length of Walk: 4 miles.
Start/finish: Castlerigg Stone Circle car park off the A591.**

Castlerigg Stone Circle was built around 1500 BC from granite not found locally. This alone makes it interesting and eerie to all ages. There are several theories as to its use but some evidence suggests that it was used by early star-gazers and also that prehistoric meetings took place here. From the parking lay-bys at Castlerigg Stone Circle walk down the road with the stones on your right. At a left bend, before Goosewell Farm, go through a gate on the right signposted The Nest. Follow the grassy footpath ahead across four fields.

The path through the last field has a wire fence on its left and open pastures on the right. It leads through a gate and into the yard of High Nest. Follow the driveway, keeping the house on the left, and walk over a cattlegrid. Directly after this turn left into a field and follow a faint path right into the corner of the field and back out to a stile and then the driveway of Low Nest. Turn right on this drive and then left on the main road. Almost immediately there is a fingerpost directing you left at a slit stile. Follow this path ahead and right a little to another slit stile in the wall. The path then veers off to the left and follows the alternating fence and wall boundary of the field.

As you pass through gate posts at the end of this field the path becomes a wider valley track. At a small footbridge there is a fingerpost. Turn left here following the sign for St John's in the Vale Church. A double-gated footbridge leads you over Naddle Beck and straight ahead to a large metal gate. A yellow arrow points you through the gate along the path. Just before another large gate the yellow arrow directs you right, across the field, towards a telegraph pole. At a finger-post near the pole turn left for St John's Church and continue along the path to a kissing gate next to a small section of solitary stone wall. Another yellow arrow can be seen on this gate.

Go through the gate and up a short, steep, rocky section ahead. Beyond this, the path is grassy and easily picks its way around the rocky outcrops with

Sykes Farm on your left. The path leads through another kissing gate to a metalled lane where you turn right and then almost immediately left up a rough, gravel lane with half of a signpost that once read St John's Church.

Continue climbing up the hair-pin bends of this lane. A small wood on the left denotes the end of the steep section. As the ground levels out underfoot, you will see another small wood on the right. Just before this wood lies a thoughtfully positioned bench just waiting to be sat on. After a short breather, continue along the lane past the Diocesan youth centre. The church that has been signposted along your route lies next door. Although built in 1845, there is written evidence that a church stood on this site as long ago as 1554. If you go through the double iron gates into the churchyard and head towards the back right corner you will see an old yew tree standing guard over a large tomb. Under the tree is a spring among the rocks with an ancient-looking metal cup chained to it, which, with a little imagination, is overflowing with legends and myths.

C.M. Isherwood

When suitable stories have been exchanged, leave the churchyard by the same gate and walk through a slit stile opposite, signposted public footpath to Tewit Tarn. This Tewit is the same as the Tewet Tarn that you're heading for. Both spellings are acceptable. Pick your way almost directly ahead to come out onto a main path after 100 yards. This stony path soon becomes a wide, green avenue cutting through bracken towards a stone wall with the rocky knoll of Low Rigg up on your left and excellent views across to St John's in the Vale on your right.

At the stone wall go through a slit stile and follow a faint path towards Tewet Tarn which is now visible ahead. Beyond the tarn the splendours of Skiddaw, on the left, and Blencathra, to the right, are on full display to tempt the more adventurous walker. At heights of 3,053ft and 2,847ft respectively, they're not on today's agenda. Climb over a stile just before the tarn and walk along the path with the tarn on your left. After some exploring here, go over a stone stile in the wall at the furthest end of the tarn.

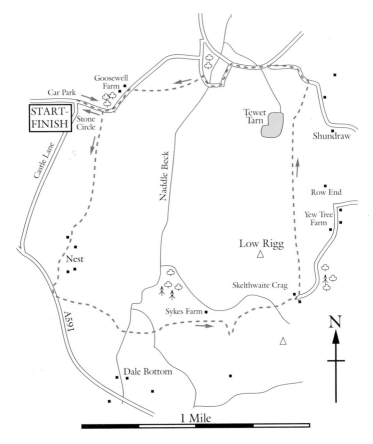

Walk straight ahead for about 200 yards to a fingerpost. Turn right here and you soon join the main, grassy track that leads downhill through a gateway in the wall. Follow the path into the bottom right corner of this field to a gate which leads onto a narrow country lane. Turn left on the lane and then left at a T-junction. At the next junction another left turn soon leads over a bridge across Naddle Beck. Just past the bridge there is a gate on the left. Go through this and then across to the right to another gate and over the adjacent ladder stile. Follow the path left towards a gate and then right by the side of a stream signposted Permissive Footpath to Castlerigg. This leads up to a stile. Go over this and turn left on the metalled road. You soon pass Goosewell Farm and the car is just around the corner on the right.

# Coledale and Barrow Door

This walk traverses peaceful valleys but gives a feeling of wild walking.
Good paths along valleys; a fairly steep first half on safe, wide paths.
Length of walk: 5 miles.
Start/finish: The first car park a third of a mile past the speed limit
sign as you leave Braithwaite towards Whinlatter Pass on the B5292.

Walk along the B5292 down the hill towards Braithwaite. Before you
actually enter the village there is a signpost for the Youth Centre Coledale,
pointing right over a small stone bridge. Cross this bridge with the lower
reaches of Coledale Beck below you and continue following the lane as it
zig-zags uphill. You may wish to call into the Coledale Inn on your right
with its Georgian bar, Victorian lounge and pleasant garden. Or maybe that
should wait until the end in case you get too comfortable.

Ignore any paths or tracks leading from this lane. Instead, continue up past
a few large, detached houses on the right to a metal gate. Climb the adjacent
stile complete with its own doggie stile. The gate is ideally positioned for
leaning on as you admire the views back over Braithwaite, Keswick and the
high fells beyond. You're now walking on a gravel track which will soon
become a wide, grassy path. The sound of Coledale Beck tumbling and
splashing below to the left may sound tempting on a hot
summer's day but there are safer descents to it later, so
resist the steep side of its valley here.

Over to the right of the path beyond a wire fence,
you will soon see the ruins of High Coledale nestled
among a small clump of trees. This was once a
remote farm and is now a likely refuge for any
small animals and birds that wish to take refuge
from the worst of the Cumbrian elements. Just
beyond this section of the path you will see the steep
hillside of Stile End looming up ahead. Fear not. The
walk avoids this ascent so you can carry on enjoying
the magnificent views to your right of the ridge
leading up to Grisedale Pike.

The forest that is visible here is Hospital Plantation, part of Whinlatter Forest Park which is very popular with families interested in walking, orienteering and nature. The forest has been shown on maps for at least 100 years but a solitary Fever Hospital was built here many years before, hence the name. Continue on the main path which lies to the left of Stile End ignoring the grassy path that forks up to the top of the fell.

Coledale Beck is still flowing to your left and the footpath quickly becomes narrower and stony. When it flattens out, take a well earned breather and enjoy impressive views ahead to Causey Pike with its finger of loose, red stone, or scree, running down one of the gullies. A real wilderness feeling exists here. Over the next 100 yards or so there are a few paths and faint tracks leading off left and right of the main stony path. Ignore them. Stay on the level main path as it takes you around the back of Stile End and then down into the next valley where Stonycroft Gill wends its way to the Newlands Valley at the bottom. Grisedale Pike can still be seen to your right in all its wild splendour.

The path soon ends at a wide, stony track where you turn left so that the stream, or gill, is on your right. This wide path soon becomes more grassy as it descends very gradually but you must still take care as there are a few steep drops to the right. The sweeping sides of Cat Bells are easily identified ahead. You are guaranteed to see walkers up there, often stretching almost the whole length of this popular fell.

The valley road is soon visible ahead as the path swings to the left above the gill. If you fancy a splash the gill is quite easy to reach if you drop down towards it near here. Back on course, the main path quickly brings you to the road. Turn left here and walk along it for about half a mile. A small wood lies ahead and you can see the path, which you will soon take from the road, to the left of the wood. Just before a bench on the right take this obvious footpath that forks off to the left. The views open out over to the right in the direction of Keswick with the bald head of Swinside poking up from the valley floor.

Continue along the path with the wood on your right. Just beyond the wood the path opens out onto a small section of broad, grassy ground with a short fingerpost  nearby. Follow the sign that leads straight ahead towards Braithwaite. The path drops down to a gate that lies between a stone wall and a wire fence. Walk through this and continue straight on across a small field and through another gate next to a footpath and bridleway fingerpost.

You are now in the farmyard of Braithwaite Lodge. Follow the lane as it passes between farm buildings and then becomes a gravel drive with the farmhouse on your right. This leads over a cattlegrid. Turn left on the road.

There is a handy village shop around the corner if you're in need of a a little sustenance. Continue along the road, across a humpback bridge over Coledale Beck. The Ivy House Hotel is on the left just past the bridge. Take the lane left in front of it and then left at the next junction. Follow this road back up to the car park.

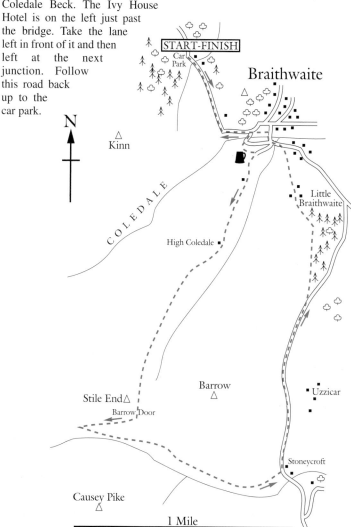

# Latrigg and Brundholme

**Latrigg is a popular destination with locals and visitors alike. For a
relatively small hill it has a superb viewpoint – with a bench at the top.
A few steep climbs; all good, clear paths and tracks
Length of walk: 5 miles.
Start/finish: Keswick Museum at Fitz Park, Station Road, Keswick.**

Walk through the iron gate by Keswick Museum and into Fitz Park. Follow
the path as it swings right, behind the museum. It curves left by the children's
play area and then passes behind a sports pavilion and eventually through a
small gate onto a lane. Turn right and follow the pavement past a few houses
until you see a rough lane on the left signposted for Skiddaw. Walk up this
lane, called Spoony Green Lane, pass over the main A66 road and soon go
through a gate situated by a house on your left. Continue through a wood as
the terrain steepens a little. There are plenty of excuses to catch your breath as
you stand and take in the views over Cat Bells, Derwent Water and Keswick
behind you. Skiddaw looms ahead with its semi-tree-covered foothill, Dodd.

The stony path soon becomes a wide, dirt track. Follow this as it hairpins left
and then right, ignoring the wide track that forks off to the right just before the
hairpins. Continue straight ahead after the right bend, passing over a small
path that cuts diagonally across the main path. Ignore another path to the right
shortly after this, near a solitary gate-post. As you leave the woods the path
swings left over a small beck and passes through a gate. You're now
surrounded by gorse and bracken with wonderful views opening out to the left
over to the Newlands fells.

The path then runs close to an enclosed evergreen wood on the left. Follow
this for about half a mile and then take the first right turn which is a wide,
stony track. This zig-zags diagonally up the fellside with splendid views
ahead. Swinside is easily identified by its bald summit above tree-covered
slopes. Beyond that is Barrow and then the massive humps of Causey Pike and
Grisedale Pike. The path now hugs the fellside and levels out a little, swinging
to the right over a small beck. Soon after this you can look down to the right
onto the track that you walked up. Eventually you reach a bench. From here
you can enjoy an almost 360 degree panoramic view over the surrounding
fells, a pretty impressive feat on such a small fell. Strictly speaking this is not

the summit. That lies behind you a short way on the gravel path that continues around the back of the bench. Once the bench has served its purpose, continue along the path climbing slightly uphill. Within a couple of minutes you will reach the summit of Latrigg at 1,203ft. The part of the 360 degree view that was missing so recently is now in view ahead, Blencathra and, in the far distance, England's backbone, the Pennines.

The level path brings you to a kissing gate and stile which you pass through or over. A solitary green path continues across the field heading right a little toward a small wood. Descend gradually with the wood lying approximately 100 yards to your left. Just before this field ends at a wire fence, the path bends down to the left and through a gate in the corner. Follow the wide track with the woods on your left. The woods soon leave the track as you continue over the field to a gate. Once through the gate turn right on a quiet country lane.

This meanders through Brundholme Wood with the sound of the River Greta gurgling below somewhere to your left. After about a mile and a quarter the lane passes over the A66 again. Continue along the lane for approximately two thirds of a mile until you approach a T-junction. A few yards before this junction take a narrow footpath on the right which follows the road around the corner to the right. This soon brings you to the road where you cross to walk on the pavement by the Briar Rigg road sign. Pass two residential roads on your left and continue past the beginning of Spoony Green Lane on your right. Retrace your steps along the main road to the small gate on the left that will take you back through Fitz Park.

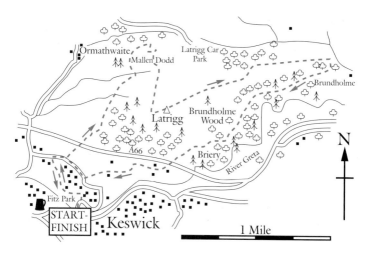

# Sale Fell

A pleasant combination of wide open spaces and mixed woodland.
Mostly broad tracks and paths; some open fellside.
Length of walk: 5 miles.
Start/finish: Parking in a lay-by at St Margaret's Church on the left,
half way between The Pheasant Inn and Wythop Mill village off the
A66 at the northern tip of Bassenthwaite Lake.

From the church walk back along the lane for about 150 yards. You will then see a public footpath Kelswick fingerpost sign to the right at a gate and adjacent kissing gate. Take this wide, green track as it climbs diagonally across the fellside. You soon pass a stone bench on the right and the track continues up to a gate in a stone wall. Go through this and, about 50 yards ahead, turn right on another green track at a T-junction.

Follow this track as it gently undulates along the open fellside for about half a mile before sweeping left. There is soon a stone wall on the right of the track and wonderful views of the smooth, grassy hump of Ling Fell ahead, slightly to the right. The track levels out here for about 100 yards. Halfway along this short, level section turn left to climb on a faint grassy path uphill, heading towards the rocky skyline ahead. After a few yards the path becomes clearer. The path soon forks. Take the right fork to continue climbing steadily upwards and onwards with the peaceful valley of Wythop to your right.

You can't go wrong now as you follow the obvious, gently undulating path along the pleasant, broad ridge. The sweeping arms of Skiddaw soon come into view across to the right with Lord's Seat dominating the rolling ridge straight across Wythop valley. Sale Fell summit is identified by its low cairn to the right of the path. The views are wonderful, particularly to Skiddaw and Bassenthwaite Lake. On a fine, clear day you can see Scotland beyond the plains on the left. From the summit cairn take a faint but wide grassy track that is seen descending to a stone wall. Go through the wide gap in this wall and over to another wall with a gap. Then take an obvious narrow path diagonally left, ignoring one that continues ahead to another cairn and one that traverses left by the wall.

Continue along the fellside and the path soon swings right, through a small dip with Wythop valley coming back into view on your right. About 100 yards out of the dip the path forks. The left fork leads up the subsidiary ridge of Lothwaite with route-finding problems at the end. So take the right fork and descend gradually on a wide track across the fellside to a wire fence. At this fence turn left along another wide track. Go through a gate at the end of this track and you are now in Wythop Wood, owned by the Forestry Commission. You may be lucky enough to see one of its shy inhabitants, the gentle roe deer.

After about 100 yards the path forks. Go right and descend gradually on a wide forest track. At a T-junction turn right again. Stay on this forest track as it hairpins left. At a right hairpin bend take a wide grassy track that bears left from the forest track at the bend. After a few hundred yards of deciduous trees, the vegetation thins out to the right to give good views over Bassenthwaite Lake and Dubwath village at the head of the lake. Ahead, you are confronted with an uninviting uphill section of the track but this isn't for you. Take the narrower path that hairpins back right from the track. The lake is now down on your left beyond trees.

This path descends slowly before steepening at a left hairpin bend. It then rolls along again with the road and lake now on your right. At a T-junction with another slightly wider path turn left. After a few yards, you reach a metalled lane with a bench on the left and a public footpath fingerpost on the right. Turn left and walk through the hamlet of Routenbeck. After approximately a third of a mile you will be back at the church.

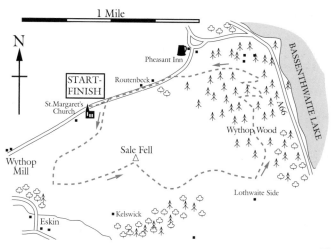

# High Rigg and St John's

This walk takes you onto a solitary ridge and is best saved for a fine day with little wind. Steep near the start; clear paths all the way with possibility of a few boggy sections particularly in valley.
Length of walk: 4½ miles.
Start/finish: Legburthwaite car park, on the B5322, off the A591 at Thirlmere.

At the end of the car park go through a gate in a low stone wall onto a narrow lane. Turn left and go through a gate at the end onto the main A591 road. Walk right for about 100 yards before climbing a ladder stile on your right. This is signposted for St John's in the Vale Church and Bridge House.

The path forks almost immediately. Take the left path and, at another fork, go left again, climbing the short, steep section ahead. The path now gently undulates before climbing through oak and pine trees. Just beyond the main cluster of trees climb another short, steep, rocky section. The stony path reverts to a grassy track with a few pine trees scattered over to the left and open fellside to the right. Another short rocky section lies ahead near the last of the pine trees. Once this has been gained you are rewarded with a magnificent view of High Rigg opening up before you. Blencathra, to the right, and Skiddaw, to the left, loom ahead on the horizon.

Continue along the grassy path and descend carefully to a gap in a stone wall ahead and then walk up the opposite side of the dip. The path soon passes through another small dip surrounded by craggy rocks that is almost an amphitheatre. The path alternates between rocky outcrops and smooth, grassy fellside and soon passes to the left of a cairn. Thirlmere Reservoir can be seen as you look back along the ridge. The villages of Armboth and Wythburn were virtually all submerged in 1894. It took 10 years to build the dam for this reservoir that was to serve Manchester. Public and environmentalists' protests could not stop it but they did help to unite people in their way of thinking. It's no coincidence that the National Trust was founded the following year.

Ahead and to the left, you can see a wire fence. It looks as though the path cuts through large rocky outcrops. However, as you approach these there is a fingerpost that diverts the footpath left just before them. Following this sign the path goes over a stile in the wire fence. The wide, green path ahead swings around to the right, gently undulating and zig-zagging.

A ladder stile over a stone wall soon shows you which way to go. Follow the path beyond it with another stone wall on your right. You will soon see a small tarn ahead next to the wall. The path leaves the wall and curves to the left of the tarn. A few faint paths criss-cross here so make sure that you follow the main one as it leads back to the side of the wall beyond the tarn.

The stone wall soon heads off to the right down the hillside. Do not follow it. Continue ahead on the main grassy path. After about 300 yards another path cuts across it just before a small dip. Ignore this and continue ahead past a tiny tarn on the left. The hillside is strewn with large boulders with one particularly big one lying about 250 yards ahead. The path passes to the right of this. About 100 yards beyond the big boulder the path swings around to the right to traverse up a short, steep, stepped section.

Follow the path straight on for a few paces then bear right and then left to bring you out on the summit of High Rigg. If that last steep section didn't take your breath away then the views probably will. Blencathra looks stunning from here. On the right lies St John's in the Vale. The ridge above it extends back to the lofty summit of Helvellyn at 3,118ft. It's believed that this mountain is the most climbed in Lakeland with crowds swarming to it most days, in all weathers. The north western fells on the left offer hard, all-day hiking to toughened walkers.

The descent path can be located to the left of the cairn where you scramble down a few yards of rock. A grassy path then leads right to a more obvious path where you bear left. The path soon becomes wide and grassy. At a fork, bear right and then quickly left to carefully climb down a grass bank, with time-worn steps cut into it, towards some buildings. The path continues downhill, through a gate and around the back of the building, the Carlisle Diocesan youth centre, to reach the lane. Turn right and walk past the church. Approximately 100 yards beyond the main gates go over a stile on the right signposted St John's in the Vale.

Follow the green lane ahead with a stone wall on your left. After about half a mile you pass through a gate and then shortly afterwards another one. The path leaves the wall for a short while but soon meets it again and you pass through a smaller gate where the wide path becomes narrower. Walk through another small gate and immediately over a beck which ducks underneath your path. You soon enter a small wood and eventually pass over another beck and gate and through to another wood. Telegraph wires are now above you. The path soon brings you to the back of Low Bridge End Farm with its hens and geese wandering the fields. There is a small tea garden here where you may welcome some refreshment.

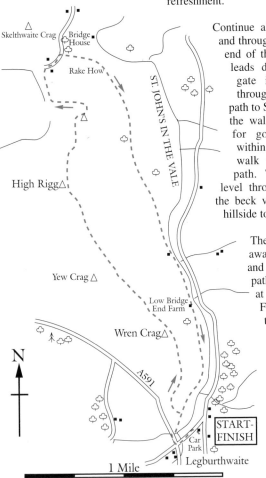

Continue along the same path and through a small gate at the end of the buildings. A path leads diagonally left to a gate in the corner. Go through this and follow the path to St John's Beck where the wall finally leaves you for good. After passing within inches of the beck, walk up a steep, gravel path. The path becomes level through woodland with the beck visible down a steep hillside to your left.

The beck soon curves away from this high path and you join the main path that you walked up at the start of the walk. Follow it back down to the ladder stile and retrace your steps to the car park.